STREET LUGE AND DIRTBOARDING

**PETER MICHALSKI
AND SUZANNE J. MURDICO**

rosen publishing's
**rosen
central**

Published in 2017 by The Rosen Publishing Group
29 East 21st Street, New York, NY 10010

Library of Congress Cataloging-in-Publication Data

Names: Michalski, Pete. | Murdico, Suzanne J.
Title: Street luge and dirtboarding / Pete Michalski and Suzanne J. Murdico.
Description: First Edition. | New York : Rosen Central, 2017. | Series:
  (Skateboarding Tips and Tricks) | Includes bibliographical references,
  webography and index. | Audience: Grades: 7-12.
Identifiers: LCCN 2016008907| ISBN 9781477788721 (Library Bound) | ISBN
  9781477788707 (Paperback) | ISBN 9781477788714 (6-pack)
Subjects: LCSH: Street luge racing--Juvenile literature. |
  Skateboarding--Juvenile literature. | Extreme sports--Juvenile literature.
Classification: LCC GV859.82 .M53 2017 | DDC 796.6/7--dc23
LC record available at http://lccn.loc.gov/2016008907

Manufactured in China

CONTENTS

INTRODUCTION

Skateboarding and snowboarding are intense sports and beloved pastimes worldwide. But sometimes skaters and snowboarders seek out alternate ways of getting that extreme sports high. Other people might not be that into skating or snowboarding to begin with but have a need for speed and excitement. For both groups, street luge and dirtboarding are exciting alternatives.

These two extreme sports have several things in common. They both have become popular in the last couple of decades, and both are somewhat close cousins of skateboarding itself.

Street luge is a hybrid of skateboarding and the winter sport called luge, a form of high-speed sledding. Dirtboarding can be thought of as almost a skateboard version of snowboarding. Both sports incorporate downhill action.

Street luge predates dirtboarding, though it remains unclear exactly when people first started. Lugeing first really caught public attention by the late 1980s and is believed to have originated on the streets of Southern California. It is also believed that downhill skaters invented street luge to go faster than was possible on regular skateboards. Lying down on boards increased the speed by cutting down on the wind resistance experienced when skaters stood (even if they crouched very low, it was still a factor).

Street luge boards resemble regular skateboards, albeit much longer. Like ice-based lugeing, street lugers lie down face up and feet first on the luge board, their bodies barely an inch above the ground. Street lugers are known as pilots. Rather than skaters' emphasis on tricks and grabbing air, street luge is a racing sport. Speed—and using it to cross the finish line before your competitors—is the goal.

Dirtboarding is also known as all-terrain boarding or mountainboarding, and it originated in the early 1990s, when snowboarding was first exploding in popularity. Snowboarders sought ways to train and stay active off-season. They wanted boards that could cover the same territory, but without the snow. So a few snowboarders decided to try modifying a skateboard. They made the board larger and replaced its small urethane (plastic) wheels with large air-filled tires.

These boards could cover uneven terrain like grass and gravel, and they could negotiate mountain trails, unlike skateboards, which required pavement. They also had the advantage of being useful year-round. It was the birth of the all-terrain board and a new sport.

CHAPTER ONE

STREET LUGE BASICS

Unlike skating or other sports, street luge is a relatively easy sport to learn. It is a dangerous sport, however, and requires practice. Protective gear is essential, especially since riders will be hitting high speeds. Racers must learn techniques for reaching top speed and for slowing down, and they must learn how to outmaneuver other racers.

GEARING UP

The good news is that street luge does not require a great deal of equipment. The bad news, though, is that the equipment is specialized and expensive. The luge itself must be light, fast, and highly durable. Protective gear is very important for keeping the rider safe and preventing injuries. When racing, luge pilots are covered from head to toe in leather to prevent road rash. They also wear helmets to protect their heads.

THE LUGE

A street luge is basically a super-modified skateboard. Bob Pereyra, the "godfather" of street luge, calls it a "skateboard on steroids." A street luge starts with the same parts as a skateboard, including a deck, wheels, and trucks. But then it is adapted for maximum speed and control.

The luge board is generally constructed of wood, steel, or aluminum. A typical sled is about 8 feet (2.4 meters) long and 16 inches (40.6 centimeters) wide, and weighs between 25 and 30 pounds (11.3 and 13.6 kilograms). But the size and weight of a sled varies depending on the height and weight of the luger, so each board must be custom made.

For certain competitions, specific rules must be followed when building a luge. For example, the sled cannot be longer than 10 feet (3 m) or weigh more than 45 pounds (20.4 kg). Also, any type of mechanical steering or brakes is forbidden.

Street luge riders use a modified version of the longboard, which itself is a variant on the classic skateboard. Due to the high speeds involved, helmets should be worn at all times.

The high speeds in this sport demand good board control. Here, Bob Pereyra accelerates on a street luge road course in Los Angeles. Pereyra has sometimes been referred to as the Godfather of Street Luge.

WHAT IS A LUGE ANYWAY?

The word "luge" means "sled" in French. Street luge is a relatively new sport. But ice luge—on which street luge is based—has been around for a long time. In fact, it's one of the oldest winter sports. It began in the winter resorts of Europe and became an Olympic sport in 1964.

The original luge is very much like street luge. It takes place on a winding downhill course. Lugers lie on their backs, feet first, on a sled and steer down the course by shifting their weight from one side to the other. The difference is that the luge course is icy rather than paved. On the smooth ice, which provides way less resistance than pavement, lugers can reach speeds of 90 miles (145 kilometers) per hour!

RIDING LEATHERS

You've probably seen street luge pilots sporting colorful leather suits when they race. These body suits come in both one-piece and two-piece varieties. You might think that racers wear skin-tight leather to look cool. But that's far from the real reason.

A leather full-body suit, known as leathers, is actually a vital part of a racer's safety gear. This thick layer of "skin" protects the luger's real skin in the event

The extreme friction that lugers can experience on their feet makes adding a layer of rubber to their shoes a good alternative to ruining a pair every time they ride.

of a crash. Some leathers have built-in knee and elbow pads for extra protection.

In addition to leather racing suits, lugers wear thick leather gloves. These gloves help protect their hands when they use them to push off at the start of a race.

PROTECT YOUR HEAD

Street luge pilots wear helmets that cover the entire head, including the face. Sometimes called brain buckets, these helmets are very similar to those worn by motorcycle riders.

Street lugers often reach the same speeds as car and motorcycle drivers. Yet the street luger's head is just inches from the pavement. That's why a full-face helmet is so important. It provides protection against serious head injuries.

The riding leathers worn by lugers are yet another protective measure that helps minimize scrapes, cuts, and gravel burns.

SHOES: WHERE THE RUBBER MEETS THE ROAD

Many street luge pilots need to replace their shoes very often. Why do shoes wear out so quickly? Street luge boards are not equipped with any brakes. The only way for pilots to slow down their sleds is to drag their feet on the asphalt, using their shoes as brakes. This friction creates an extreme heat. Talk about burning rubber!

Most street lugers wear athletic shoes with thick rubber soles. Even so, the rubber sometimes burns right through to the soles of their feet! That's why some lugers attach pieces of rubber from old car tires to the bottoms of their shoes. This added layer helps prevent the shoes from wearing out so quickly.

BOARDER BIO: PAMELA ZOOLALIAN

At first glance, Pamela Zoolalian doesn't look much like a street luger. For one, she's a woman in a sport dominated by men. For another, she's only 5 feet 2 inches tall and weighs just 110 pounds. That's tiny compared with her competitors. Some of them are over 6 feet tall and outweigh her by 140 pounds!

But Zoolalian uses her size to her advantage in luge racing. Although she often gets off to a slow start, she gains speed during the race. Her small size allows her to more easily maneuver tight turns than her larger competitors. Being small also helps Zoolalian squeeze between other lugers in the pack. And her specialty is pulling off the draft created by the other pilots.

Continued on page 12

Continued from page 11

Whatever Pamela Zoolalian might be lacking in size, she more than makes up for with attitude and style. Not only does she dye her hair pink, she also wears bright pink leathers when she races. She even rides a pink luge!

In a *New York Times* interview, Zoolalian was asked about all the pink. "I just wanted to make sure people knew that there was a girl out there kicking butt," she answered. "And most guys, unless they're really confident, wouldn't go head-to-toe pink."

Just in case other lugers still don't notice Zoolalian, the back of her helmet reads, "Spanked by a chick." That way, when she whizzes past her competitors, they'll know who beat them to the finish line!

LUGE RACING

Luge racing takes place on a long downhill course. The course is most often a regular street that has been closed to traffic. It may be anywhere from 2 miles to 12 miles (3.2 to 19.3 km) long and usually has many twists and turns. Courses are generally lined with bales of hay to act as cushions in case lugers crash on a curve.

ON YOUR MARKS

At the start of a race, lugers line up at the paddle apron. This area is usually at the top of a long downhill street. Here, racers use their hands to "paddle," or push themselves forward. This is the only time lugers are allowed to use their hands. Size and strength are major advantages during this first stage of a race.

Larger pilots usually have greater power, allowing them to get off to a faster start than smaller pilots.

After the initial paddling, gravity starts to take over and the luge begins to gather speed as it heads downhill. Although they are lying down, luge pilots must raise their heads slightly to see where they're going. To steer, they use subtle shifts of their bodies.

SPEED, STRATEGY, AND TECHNIQUE

Lugeing may look like it's all about raw speed. Pilots routinely reach speeds of 60 to 70 miles per hour (96–112 km/h). Some luge pilots have even clocked in at more than 80 miles per hour (128 km/h). That's faster than cars traveling on a highway!

Although speed is very important, lugeing also involves strategy and technique. Luge pilots generally use one of two main racing strategies during competition. Some pilots choose to start quickly, paddling fast and furious to get to the front of the pack. Once in the lead, they have only to maintain their position to win the race.

But luge pilots using the second racing strategy try to take away that lead at the last minute. These pilots hang back to take advantage of the draft created by the lead racers. The pilots in front have already broken through the wind barrier. This makes it easier for the pilots in the back to gather speed. Drafting racers then attempt to make a quick pass to the front just before the finish line.

HITTING THE BRAKES

When racing through a tight corner, luge pilots must slow down to avoid a crash. But street luges have no brakes. This makes slowing down a speeding luge a bit tricky!

There are two basic ways to brake. One way is to use foot power—dragging your feet across the pavement. The other way to slow down is by sitting further upright on the luge. This makes the sled less aerodynamic because it increases the wind resistance. Many luge racers use a combination of these two.

At the end of a race or practice run, lugers often need to stop quickly. One popular technique is called stoppies or quickstop. The luger plants his or her feet flat on the ground, lifts the front of the board, and stands up at the same time.

PRACTICE MAKES PERFECT

Most lugers would probably agree that one of the most difficult aspects of the sport is finding a place to practice. Lugeing is normally done on a paved surface with a steep incline. The problem is that most paved surfaces are roads filled with cars.

Traffic can make lugeing extremely dangerous. For safety reasons, luge racers often practice together. A car usually follows a pilot down the hill during practice runs. This prevents other cars from crashing into the luger.

For most luge pilots, the best places to practice are mountain roads. Good lugeing roads offer steep hills where racers can reach high speeds. They also provide curves and bends. And, most important, these roads have little traffic. Many professional luge pilots live in California, where these roads are fairly common.

"Nothing handles like a luge on a mountain road," says John Frey. Frey is a street luge pilot who has raced at many competitions, including the X Games. "The sheer speed, the draft—every little part of it gives me a rush," he told *Louisville Magazine.* "To hit 80 miles per hour on one of these things is so unbelievable," he added. "It's just like you're on a cushion of air."

"CLASSIC" LUGE

One offshoot of street luge is known as classic luge, often referred to as "buttboard," named after the simplified version of a street luge board it employs. This board more closely resembles a piece of wood with wheels, or a very rough-looking basic skateboard. Because many new and also established lugers make and customize their own sleds, the simpler design of the buttboard allows beginners to start learning the sport more cheaply and easily. Wood buttboards are slower and easier to learn luge on than steel or fiberglass sleds and are usually much cheaper, too. This allows riders to check out the sport without investing a substantial amount of money. Many people who are hooked on classic luge move on to regular street luge or enjoy and compete in both.

Rules established among classic luge aficionados prevent riders from overengineering or making their boards too fancy. Decks are limited to 48 inches (122 cm) long and 12 inches (30.5 cm) wide. Wheels are limited to 70mm (2.75 inches) or less.

One famous street luge fan was Darren Lott, a street luge champion who established what a standard board for classic luge would look like. This is still referred to by many as a "Lott Classic." He also worked hard to promote the sport as a part of the larger "gravity sports" world.

CHAPTER TWO

STREET LUGE: EVENTS AND COMPETITIONS

Street luge competitions and events are held throughout the year. They are usually sponsored by downhill skateboarding and street luge organizations and sometimes are part of larger extreme sports gatherings. Street luge experienced a burst of popularity in the 1990s and through the 2000s, when its popularity leveled off. It has continued to thrive, especially overseas. Two major competitions that increased its popularity in the United States and internationally were the X Games and the Gravity Games, each held once a year and televised to millions of viewers around the world.

The last Gravity Games were held in 2006. While the X Games continue, street luge ceased to be part of the competition.

X GAMES

The X Games are the Olympics of extreme sports, sponsored by ESPN, the cable television sports network. Started in 1995, they are now held twice each year. At the Winter X

Games, athletes compete in such sports as snowboarding and skiing. The Summer X Games include contests in skateboarding, downhill BMX, and aggressive inline skating.

The street luge event made its debut at the first X Games competition in 1995. Few people until then were familiar with it. Televised street luge events made them want to find out more about this exciting new sport.

Street lugers from around the world participated in the X Games. They competed for gold, silver, and bronze medals and for prize money.

A competitor takes a spill during a competition. Chances are you will fall or lose control at some point. Stay alert and learn how to do so safely.

Over the years, the types of street luge events held at the X Games changed. At the first two X Games, there were just two street luge contests—dual downhill and mass downhill. In 1997, super mass downhill was added to the lineup. In later years, the mass and dual events were discontinued. But in 2000, a new contest—king of the hill—showcased the best street luge racers at the X Games.

DUAL DOWNHILL

The dual event featured one-on-one races between two lugers. Timed qualifying rounds determined the sixteen fastest athletes. These racers then faced off against each other in eight paired races. The winner of each contest advanced to the next round, and the loser was eliminated. Rounds continued until the two fastest lugers competed for the gold and silver medals. Races were often won or lost by mere fractions of a second.

MASS AND SUPER MASS DOWNHILL

The mass and super mass competitions involved larger groups of lugers than the dual. Mass and super mass both began with racers each taking two qualifying runs that were timed. Lugers received an overall ranking based on these runs. Those racers with the fastest times qualified for competition.

In the mass event, lugers competed in four-person heats. Racers sped down city streets, sometimes reaching 70 miles per hour or more. After each mass race, the top two lugers advanced to the next round. In super mass, each heat had six lugers. The top three advanced.

In the mass event, the final race featured the top four competitors. In super mass, the finals involved the top six competitors.

Street luge competition heats with many participants can be very intense, especially at high speeds. The more racers there are, the more each competitor needs to be wary of crashing into a fellow luger.

In both events, the first three finishers received gold, silver, and bronze medals.

KING OF THE HILL

The first king of the hill competition was held at the 2000 X Games. In this event, all street luge gold medal winners from the previous X Games competed against one another. This competition was run like the super mass event. The winner was pronounced the King of the Hill.

The king of the hill competition was supposed to be a one-time-only event at the 2000 X Games. But it was so popular that a second king of the hill event was held the following year. Dennis Derammelaere became the first King of the Hill at the 2000 X Games. He went on to reclaim his crown at the 2001 X Games.

BIKER SHERLOCK: A STREET LUGE AND EXTREME SPORTS LEGEND AND ENTREPRENEUR

Biker Sherlock, who passed away in late 2015, established himself as a famous name in street luge. He won seven medals in street luge at the X Games—four gold, two silver, and one bronze. He also performed well at the Gravity Games, winning one gold and two silver medals in street luge. He was even one of the organizers of the Gravity Games, which showcased extreme sports from 1999 to 2006.

Michael Sherlock was born in New Jersey. Growing up, he was nicknamed "Biker" because of his love for riding dirt bikes. A friend introduced him to street lugeing in 1995. Less than a year later, Sherlock entered his first professional competition—the 1996 X Games. To everyone's surprise, he won the gold medal.

Sherlock participated in many other extreme sports. These included surfing, snowboarding, wakeboarding, motocross, and mountain biking.

Sherlock was more than just an extreme athlete, though. He was also a businessman, having been the owner and president of Extreme Downhill International (EDI). EDI organized and promoted downhill skateboarding and street luge events. Sherlock also owned a company that sells street luge equipment and skateboards, Dregs Skateboards.

GRAVITY GAMES

The Gravity Games were network television's answer to the X Games. Shown on NBC, the Gravity Games featured competitions similar to those at the X Games. The Gravity Games were held from 1999 to 2006 and included two street luge events. In the four-man event, four racers competed in each heat. The six-man event involved six competitors. The first racer to cross the finish line won the heat. The winners of each heat then competed for the gold, silver, and bronze medals.

Street luge legend Biker Sherlock (*right*) leads another competitor during a four-man street luge competition during the Gravity Games in Providence, Rhode Island, in September 2001.

MODERN STREET LUGE COMPETITION

These days, street luge remains popular, even if its practitioners ride a bit more under the radar. Other nations have embraced the sport, while North American events, meet-ups, and competitions take place throughout the year. Two organizations serve as governing bodies for street luge (and related sports), which means they set the rules and standards by which riders compete, organize events, hand out prizes, and maintain official rankings of riders worldwide. These are the International Downhill Federation (IDF) and the International Gravity Sports Association (IGSA).

Street lugers still participate in mass runs, with up to twenty racers competing at a time or competing in different heats, such as in super mass and other configurations of the event. Dual downhill remains popular, as do king of the hill–type contests. Another form of street luge competition is the endurance race, in which competitors ride a course that is several miles long.

CHAPTER THREE

THE BASICS OF DIRTBOARDING

Dirtboarding may not be as big as snowboarding, but it has some advantages over similar and related sports. For one thing, it can be done almost anywhere, in almost any kind of environment. Dirtboarders can ride during any season, too. Many dirtboarders prefer any kind of rocky or elevated terrain in nature.

Snowboarding is limited to winter months in areas with snow. Wakeboarding is limited to summer months in areas with water. But it's possible to dirtboard from January through December and in just about any climate. It can be done on almost any type of terrain and requires no snow, water, or wind.

Dirtboards handle much like snowboards. Many snowboarders ride dirtboards in the off-season. Rather than carving the snow, dirtboarders carve the dirt. They often ride at the same locations where they snowboard when there's snow on the ground.

But dirtboards are also similar enough to skateboards that many skateboarders enjoy riding them. Many of the tricks that can be performed on a skateboard can also be done on a dirtboard.

As with any sport, safety is a concern. But dirtboarding is probably no more dangerous than other extreme sports. The key to preventing injuries is to start slowly and follow safety guidelines.

Dirtboards—also known as mountainboards—are distinctive due to their extra-large tires and larger size compared to standard skateboards.

CHOOSING A DIRTBOARD

Dirtboards come in a variety of styles and sizes. Most dirtboards are about the same length as snowboards but are longer than regular skateboards. Different types of dirtboards are available for different types of terrain— from smooth pavement to grassy slopes to steep rocky cliffs.

A dirtboard has the same basic parts as a skateboard—a deck, trucks, and wheels. But on dirtboards, these parts have been modified for all terrains, not just pavement. Dirtboards also have a suspension system, or shock absorbers. This system is designed to soften bumps when riding over rough terrain.

DIRTBOARD DECKS

Just as on a skateboard, the platform part of the dirtboard—where the rider stands—is called the deck. Most decks are made of several layers of laminated wood. This type of construction makes the boards tough yet flexible.

Like snowboards, dirtboard decks are equipped with bindings to hold the rider's feet in place. Bindings allow riders to catch air and carve hard while staying attached to the board. Dirtboard bindings may be adjustable straps, or they may be fixed metal bars. In either case, riders can move their feet in and out easily. That way, they can release themselves from the board if they should fall.

TRUCKS

The trucks are axles that are attached to the bottom of the board—one in the front and one in the rear. The trucks hold the wheels in place. They also hold dampeners that work as shock absorbers on rough terrain. When the rider pivots from side to side, the shock absorbers allow for smooth motion.

WHEELS

Dirtboard wheels are very different from standard skateboard wheels.

Getting on a dirtboard for the first time can be exciting, but remember to take it seriously and stay safe.

Instead of small plastic wheels, dirtboards have large pneumatic, or inflated, tires. These tires are very similar to those used on dirt bikes.

Plastic skateboard wheels travel well only on smooth surfaces. But dirtboard tires are large enough to roll over small obstacles without getting stuck. They allow travel on any type of terrain—from flat asphalt to bumpy mountain trails.

BOARDER: JASON LEE

You may not be familiar with Jason Lee (not to be confused with the former pro skater turned film and television actor with the same name). But without him, all-terrain boarding might not even exist today. Lee is considered by many to be the pioneer of the sport.

In the early 1990s, Jason Lee was an avid skier and snowboarder. But the skiing and snowboarding season is fairly short—lasting only until the snow melts. Lee wanted to find an extreme sport like snowboarding, but one that could be done in the off-season.

So Lee and his friend Patrick McConnell decided to create a new type of board. This one could be ridden on the same mountain terrain as skis and snowboards but didn't require snow. Lee and McConnell took a skateboard deck but replaced the wheels with off-road tires, similar to mountain bike tires. The pair also added a suspension system for a smoother ride.

When people saw Lee and McConnell testing their new boards, they became curious and wanted to try it themselves. Not only were skiers and snowboarders interested but also surfers and skateboarders. In 1993, Lee and McConnell started their own company—MBS Mountainboards—to manufacture and sell the new boards. Today, several other companies also produce all-terrain boards.

Jason Lee also competed in many mountainboarding contests and won several world championships. And he has appeared on television many times—being interviewed about the sport and riding a mountainboard in commercials for Nissan. Jason Lee even holds a place in the *Guinness Book of World Records* as the person with the most mountainboarding titles.

SAFETY FIRST

By now, you know that dirtboarding can be dangerous. That's part of the reason why it's so exciting! Safety is absolutely crucial. Playing it safe today will help you get back on your board tomorrow.

As you gain confidence on the dirtboard, you will want to try more daring and aerial manuevers.

SNOWBOARDING'S ORIGINS

The inspiration for dirtboarding came from snowboarding. Snowboarding is a winter sport that was developed in the United States during the 1960s. Snowboarders carve the snow on a board that's similar to a skateboard with no wheels. Snowboarding combines elements of skiing, surfing, and skateboarding.

Many people credit Sherman Poppen with the invention of the snowboard. In 1965, Poppen was looking to create a fun new toy for his daughter. He bound two skis together and added a rope for steering. Calling it the "snurfer"—a combination of snow and surfer—Poppen marketed the first snowboard.

Over the years, snowboard designs were modified and improved. And by 1990, snowboarding had become one of the most popular winter sports in the United States. Snowboarding debuted as an official Olympic sport at the 1998 Olympic Winter Games in Nagano, Japan. Its inclusion in the Olympics helped snowboarding become accepted as a true competitive sport, not just a fad.

CHECK THE TERRAIN

In any extreme sport, falls are inevitable—even for experienced athletes. Falling from a skateboard onto the pavement can be painful. Snowboard falls can hurt, too. Even though new-fallen snow is soft, packed or icy snow makes for hard landings.

But dirtboard terrain can be tough, too. The surface might be covered with tree roots, gravel, rocks, or other sharp objects. Keep in mind that you're traveling downhill fast. The faster you're going, the harder you'll fall. As one ski resort director put it, "Mountainboarding is not a contact sport. It's a contact-with-the-ground sport."

Before stepping onto a board, check out the terrain where you plan to ride. Beginning dirtboarders should look for gentle grassy slopes and steer clear of steep hills and areas with bumps or rocks. Even advanced dirtboarders should survey the area before taking a ride. It's always better to be aware of obstacles and potential problem spots.

PROTECT YOURSELF: GEARING UP

No matter what type of board you use or where you ride, you can still get hurt if you fall. Wearing protective gear will help prevent serious injuries. For dirtboarding, a helmet, elbow pads, and knee pads are musts. Gloves, wrist guards, butt pads, and eye protection are also highly recommended.

Some all-terrain boards come equipped with brakes. The brakes usually have hand controls. These types of boards are especially useful for beginners who are learning how to stop.

Dirtboard riders should also be mindful not only of fellow riders, but also onlookers (especially during competitions), as well as passerby moving through any chosen terrain. These can include hikers or other extreme sports enthusiasts like dirt bikers. Accidents can occur, and a falling rider coming down a hill could even potentially kill someone at the bottom—not to mention dirtboarders getting hurt themselves. Steep terrain can also

Female competitors board downhill through a dirt course during a competition, kicking up dust in their wake, as onlookers take pictures and video footage.

transform a runaway board into a weapon. Many venues and resorts that allow or promote dirtboarding will require a leash or other measure to attach boards to their riders.

CHAPTER FOUR

DIRTBOARDING: GETTING STARTED

Dirtboarding aficionados differ among themselves in just how, exactly, they got into the sport. They may have had friends who are riders and were curious. Others were already skateboarders, were fans of gravity sports, or came from the world of BMX freestyle. Snowboarders seem to be the most likely fans to get into dirtboarding since the sports are so similar. If you already do any of these sports, you are ahead of the game. If not, don't worry; it's fun just learning.

CHOOSE A BOARD

Dirtboards are sold in many skate and surf shops and some sporting goods stores. Deciding which dirtboard is right for you will depend on your age, height, weight, and ability.

Ask yourself: how and where do you plan to ride? Are you looking for a fast but stable ride? Or do you want to perform lots of turns and tricks? Do you like rough, bumpy terrain, or smooth surfaces, like snow or ice?

In general, heavy-duty boards are built to handle the abuse of extreme terrain. Lighter weight boards are better for freestyle riding involving stunts and tricks. However, several factors affect the performance and ride of a dirtboard.

- **Board Length.** Dirtboards are available in a variety of sizes. Longer boards allow greater speed while maintaining stability. Shorter boards are better suited for maneuvering tight turns and performing tricks.

- **Tires.** Dirtboard tires vary widely in style and size, depending on the intended terrain. In addition to tire size—which ranges from about nine to twelve inches in diameter—the amount of air in the tires also affects the ride: hard, full tires for high speeds, softer ones for a slower, smoother ride.

- **Bindings.** Dirtboard bindings are available in two main types. Soft bindings are made of Velcro and can be loosened or tightened for different shoes or different riders. Freestyle bindings, or hard foot rails, are sturdier but not adjustable. Both types of bindings, however, keep your feet planted firmly on the board.

LEARN TO RIDE

A good way to try out dirtboarding is to rent a board. Skate shops and ski resorts that allow dirtboarding during summer months rent out boards. Some even come with instructional videos for riders.

Most dirtboards cost several hundred dollars, so it's a smart idea to try before you buy. Renting allows you to test different boards to find the right one. If you decide to buy a dirtboard, some shops will even put your rental fee toward the board's purchase price.

STARTING OUT: THE BASICS

Before riding, put on all of your safety gear, including a helmet. Experts recommend that beginning riders start on a flat surface. Long before attempting downhill riding, you need to practice stopping. Knowing how to stop will help prevent serious injuries.

When you're ready to try riding downhill, start with a slightly inclined terrain, not a steep one. Also, keep your tire pressure low. Lower tire pressure will keep the dirtboard moving more slowly. This gives you greater control over the speed of your descent.

SPEED AND TURNS

After you have mastered a slight incline, you might want to try a somewhat sharper one. The average speed for dirtboarding is between 10 and 12 miles per hour (16–19 km/h). You can control your speed not only by adjusting your tire pressure but also by making turns.

Turning on a dirtboard is very similar to snowboard turning. It requires alternate pressure from the heels and toes. On a sharp curve, your hand can skim the ground to maintain balance.

With patience and practice, you can become an accomplished dirtboard rider. You can learn how to ride downhill, carve the dirt, and catch big air. You might even want to try some basic tricks, such as grabs. Many dirtboard tricks are nearly identical to those done on snowboards.

Avoid getting overcnfident on a dirtboard the first few times you try it out, even if you have experience skating or snowboarding. You could easily find yourself rolling out of control downhill if you are not careful.

Once you gain confidence as a dirtboarder, you can start using your arms and playing with your balance to pull off different tricks.

PICKING YOUR TERRAIN

During their off-season, many ski resorts are open to dirtboarders, mountain bikers, and other extreme sports enthusiasts. At these locations, dirtboarders can carve dirt on the same slopes where snowboarders carve snow in the winter.

Some ski resorts promote dirtboarding by offering how-to clinics for beginners. Many resorts even allow dirtboarders to use the ski lifts. Instead of having to carry their boards up the hill, dirtboarders can take the lift back to the top after a downhill run.

Aside from ski resorts, there are plenty of places to "do the dirt." Parks, dirt roads, uncrowded hiking or bike trails, and BMX tracks are a few examples. Just be sure to read and obey posted signs. Also, remember to respect public and private property, as well as the people and vehicles around you.

COMPETITIONS

For many experienced dirtboarders, part of the sport's enjoyment is competing against other riders. Like snowboarding and skate-boarding contests, dirtboarding events involve testing speed and

As you get proficient at dirtboarding, you can start to really let loose and catch some air. Doing so is not only fun, but it helps you clear obstacles better and gain speed while racing.

skill and performing big tricks. There are a variety of dirtboard competitions, including the following:

- **Boardercross**—A racing competition in which dirtboarders face off in a head-to-head match. Racers compete on a downhill dirt course filled with turns and jumps.
- **Freestyle**—A competition involving tricks. The main focus is on performing a variety of stunts and catching big air.

KITEBOARDING

The latest trend in all-terrain boarding is called kiteboarding or kite surfing. Instead of gravity power, kiteboarders use wind power to propel them. The idea behind kiteboarding came from windsurfing. Windsurfers ride over ocean waves on a surfboard with a sail attached to it.

Kiteboarders use rope lines to attach large kites or lightweight parachutes to a control bar. The kites are flown like regular kites. But kiteboarders hold onto the kite lines while riding on their dirtboards. As the wind pulls the kite, the kite boarder is pulled over all types of terrain.

It's much easier to sail downwind than upwind, so most beginning kiteboarders travel that way. Experts in the sport, however, can travel upwind and even perform jumps. They use the kite to lift them off the ground and gently drop them back down again. Some can jump 10 feet (3 m) high and travel 100 feet (30 m) in the air before returning to the ground.

- **Big air**—A competition for best trick. Each rider gets several runs to perform one big trick and attempt to stick the landing.
- **Downhill**—A test of speed. Dirtboarders line up at the top of a hill and race down to the bottom. The winner is the first person to cross the finish line.

A kiteboarder (not to be confused with those who do the watersport by the same name) gets some major air behind his parachute.

THE FUTURE FOR DIRTBOARDING

What does the future hold for dirtboarding/mountainboarding? Will the sport ever become as popular as snowboarding? Bruce Adams, owner of a Colorado skateboard shop, seems to think so. "Right now, mountainboarding is really in its infancy," says Adams. "Down the road, I think [mountainboards are] gonna be as big as snowboards are because it gives the snowboarders a way to carve all year."

GLOSSARY

aerodynamic Designed to reduce wind resistance and increase speed.

bindings Straps on a dirtboard that keep the rider's feet in place.

buttboard A board used in classic luge, as opposed to the luge of standard street luge.

carve To make a dirtboard turn in an arc by leaning hard in one direction.

classic luge A version of street luge using a smaller and cheaper board, replacing the sled.

deck The platform of a dirtboard.

drafting A strategy in which a racer tucks behind another racer, taking advantage of the air pocket created to gather speed.

leathers Leather body suits worn by luge pilots to help prevent road rash.

luge A sled made for racing; a street luge has wheels and is raced on pavement, while an ice luge has no wheels and is raced on packed snow.

luge pilot An athlete who races luges.

paddle apron The area at the start of a luge race in which pilots push themselves forward with their arms.

pneumatic Describes something filled with air, such as a tire.

road rash Burns created when skin scrapes the road surface.

sled Another name for a luge board.

terrain The physical features of a piece of land.

truck Axle on the bottom of a dirtboard that holds the wheels in place.

wind resistance The pressure of the air against a luge pilot.

All Terrain Boarding Association (ATBA)
39 Cotswold Avenue
Rayleigh, Essex SS6 8AN
England
Website: http://www.atbaonline.com
The All Terrain Boarding Association (ATBA) is the governing body for mountainboarding in the United Kingdom. The association aims to promote the growth of the sport.

International Downhill Federation (IDF)
Website: http://www.internationaldownhillfederation.org
The International Downhill Federation (IDF) is one of two official governing bodies of gravity sports, representing international downhill skateboard, street luge, and classic luge. The federation coordinates and ensures the safety of downhill racing events internationally.

International Gravity Sports Association (IGSA)
638 North Crestview Drive
Glendora, CA 91741
(626) 963-5304
Website: http://www.igsaworldcup.com
The International Gravity Sports Association (IGSA) was formed in 1996 by a group of downhill skateboarding and street luge enthusiasts to foster strong and fair competition, establish rules, and administer competitions.

MBS Mountainboards
212 Sutton Lane
Colorado Springs, CO 80907
(719) 884-1000
Website: http://www.mbs.com
Founded in 1993, MBS pioneered the original mountainboards for
    purchase and use by participants in the then emerging sport.

WEBSITES

Because of the changing nature of Internet links, Rosen
Publishing has developed an online list of websites related to the
subject of this book. This site is updated regularly. Please use this
link to access this list:

http://www.rosenlinks.com/STT/luge

Brooke, Michael. *The Concrete Wave: The History of Skateboarding*. Toronto, ON: Warwick Publishing, 1999.

Caitlin, Stephen. *Skateboard Fun*. Mahwah, NJ: Troll Communications, 1998.

Choyce, Lesley. *Skateboard Shakedown*. Halifax, NS: Formac, 1989.

Doeden, Matt. *Skateparks: Grab Your Skateboard*. Mankato, MN: Capstone Press, 2002.

Gaines, Ann Graham. *The Composite Guide to Extreme Sports*. Philadelphia, PA: Chelsea House Publishers, 2000.

Hawk, Tony. *Hawk: Occupation: Skateboarder*. New York, NY: Reagan Books, 2000.

Kamberg, Mary-Lane. *Dirtboarding* (Skateboarding Tips and Tricks). New York, NY: Rosen Publishing, 2016.

Loizos, Constance. *Extreme Sports Skateboard!: Your Guide to Street, Vert, Downhill, and More*. Des Moines, IA: National Geographic Children's Books, 2002.

Lott, Darren. *Street Luge Survival Guide*. Irvine, CA: Gravity Publishing, 1998.

Marcus, Ben. *The Skateboard: The Good, the Rad, and the Gnarly*. Minneapolis, MN: MVP Books/Lerner Publishing, 2011.

Nichols, John. *Street Luge*. Austin, TX: Raintree Steck-Vaughn Publishers, 2002.

Preszler, Eric. *Mountainboarding* (X-Sports). Mankato, MN: Capstone Press, 2005.

Ryan, Pat. *Extreme Skateboarding*. Mankato, MN: Capstone Press, 1998.

Ryan, Pat. *Street Luge Racing.* Mankato, MN: Capstone Press, 1998.

Sohn, Emily. *Skateboarding: How It Works* (The Science of Sports – Sports Illustrated for Kids). Mankato, MN: Capstone Publishers, 2010.

Youngblut, Shelly, ed. *Way Inside ESPN's X Games.* New York, NY: Hyperion/ESPN Books, 1998.

Welinder, Per, and Pete Whitely. *Mastering Skateboarding.* Champaign, IL: Human Kinetics, 2011.

Beyette, Beverly. "Go, Street Luge Racer." *Los Angeles Times*, June 5, 2000.

Carpenter, Susan. "Dirtheads and Good Air Days." *Los Angeles Times*, August 6, 2001.

"Derring Dude." *People,* January 12, 1998 (http://www.people .com/people/archive/article/0,,20124212,00.html).

Dizon, Kristen. "Mountainboards Let You Carve Hills, Trails, Even City Parks and Streets Year-round." *Seattle Post-Intelligencer*, August 7, 2000.

EXPN.com. "Street Luge Events" (http://xgames.espn.go.com /xgames).

Flatley, Kate. "Street Luge: Tough Sledding, No Ice." *Wall Street Journal*, September 30, 1997 (http://www.wsj.com /articles/SB875572481833917000).

Gorant, Jim. "All Aboard!" *Popular Mechanics*, November 1997.

"Gravity Fest Racing Saturday, Sunday in Munnsville." *Oneida Dispatch*, July 28, 2015 (http://www.oneidadispatch.com/ article/OD/20150728/NEWS/150729745).

Halpin, Peter. "Surfin' C.O." *Boulder Weekly*, June 8, 2000.

Hoenig, Henry. "Going to Extremes." *Louisville Magazine*, June 1998.

Mongoose ATB. "What Is Kite Surfing?" (http://www.mongoose-atb.com/kite.html).

MSNBC.com. "Mountainboarding: High on Thrills" (http://www. msnbc.com/news/433811.asp).

Robertson, Les. "Rest in Peace: Biker Sherlock, Downhill Legend." Skate Slate, December 4, 2015 (http://www.

skateslate.com/blog/2015/12/04
/rest-in-peace-biker-sherlock-downhill-legend).

Tauber, Chris. "Extremely Pink." *New York Times Upfront*,
October 1, 2001.

Way Inside ESPN's X Games. New York, NY: Hyperion/ESPN
Books, 1998.

INDEX

ABOUT THE AUTHORS

Peter Michalski is a young adult nonfiction author who has penned many instructional titles for teens, covering sports, careers, and health issues.

Suzanne J. Murdico is a published author of children's books and young adult books. Some of her published works include *Osama Bin Laden* (Middle East Leaders), *Earthquakes: A Practical Survival Guide* (The Library of Emergency Preparedness), and *In-line Skating: Techniques and Tricks* (Rad Sports).

PHOTO CREDITS

Cover, p. 10 Purestock/Getty Images; pp. 1, 6, 16, 23, 31 Liushengfilm/Shutterstock.com; p. 3 Dizzo/Vetta/Getty Images; pp. 4-5 mgs/Moment Open/Getty Images; p. 7 Doug Pensinger/ Getty Images Sport/Getty Images; p. 8 Mike Powell/Getty Images; pp. 9, 19, 35 © Buzz Pictures/Alamy Stock Photo; p. 17 Robert Cianflone/Getty Images; p. 21 © AP Images p. 24 Chris Herbrand/Gamma-Rapho/Getty Images; p. 25 Ingram Publishing/Getty Images; p. 27 Jeff Morgan 07/Alamy Stock Photo; p. 30 © Will Newitt/Alamy Stock Photo; p. 34 Klubovy/E+/Getty Images; p. 36 © Adrian Sheratt/Alamy Stock Photo; p. 38 © Stephen James Wakeling/Alamy Stock Photo; back cover, interior pages (bricks) Ensuper/Shutterstock.com; interior pages banner textures Naburalna/Shutterstock.com

Designer: Michael Moy; Editor: Philip Wolny;
Photo Researcher: Karen Huang and Philip Wolny